WHO WERE THE
VIKINGS?

First published in 2006
in the UK by Franklin Watts
338 Euston Road, London NW1 3BH

Franklin Watts Australia, Hachette Children's Books
Level 17/207 Kent Street, Sydney NSW 2000

This series was devised and produced by McRae Books Srl,
Borgo S. Croce, 8, Florence (Italy)
Text: Anne McRae
Main Illustrations: Lorenzo Cecchi, Valeria Ferretti, Giacinto Gaudenzi, Alessandro Menchi, MM comunicazione (Manuela Cappon, Monica Favilli), Francesca D'Ottavi, Paola Ravaglia, Sergio
Illustrations: Studio Stalio (Alessandro Cantucci, Fabiano Fabbrucci, Margherita Salvadori)
Design: Marco Nardi

Colour separations: Fotolito Toscana, Florence (Italy)

© 2006 McRae Books Srl, Florence
All rights reserved. No part of this book may be reproduced, stored in a retrieval system or transmitted in any form or by any means, electronic, mechanical, photocopying or otherwise, without the prior written permission of the copyright holder.

A CIP catalogue record for this book is available from the British Library.
Dewey Decimal Classification Number: 948'.022

ISBN-10: 0 7496 6789 3
ISBN-13: 978 0 7496 6789 4

Printed and bound in Italy.

WHO WERE THE VIKINGS?

FRANKLIN WATTS
LONDON • SYDNEY

Feasting and Fun
see pages 26-27

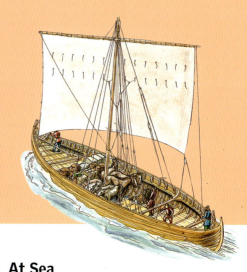

At Sea
see pages 12-13

Contents

Who were the Vikings?	6–7	Feasting and Fun	26–27
Viking Origins	8–9	Writing and Myths	28–29
Viking Raiders	10–11	End of the Viking Age	30–31
At Sea	12–13	Index	32
Travel and Trade	14–15		
Farmers and Food	16–17		
Gods and Goddesses	18–19		
Burials	20–21		
Daily Life	22–23		
Towns	24–25		

Towns
see pages 24-25

Viking Raiders
see pages 10-11

Shipbuilding
see page 13

Astute Traders

Scandinavia was rich in raw materials, such as furs, timber and amber, and the Vikings traded these goods all over Europe. Viking traders travelled in boats by sea and river.

Great Seafarers

The Vikings crossed the Atlantic Ocean in their sturdy, well-built boats and arrived in North America a good 500 years before Christopher Columbus set sail.

Long-distance Trade
see page 15

Skilled Artisans

Viking craftspeople worked in metal, ivory, wood and stone to create jewellery, like this brooch, and to decorate household utensils and furniture. Designs often included intertwined stylized animals.

An ornate bronze, silver and gold brooch.

 Grave Goods see page 21

Fearsome Warriors

The Vikings are mostly remembered as savage raiders because, for about 300 years, they terrorized Britain and the rest of Europe with wave after wave of violent attacks. This time is known as the Viking Age.

 Targets see page 10

This carving shows Viking raiders at the abbey of Lindisfarne.

Who were the Vikings?

The Vikings were a Scandinavian people who lived in the modern-day countries of Denmark, Sweden and Norway. They spoke Old Norse, from which the modern languages of Scandinavia are descended. At the end of the 8th century, the Vikings began to raid Britain and other countries in Europe. At first they simply plundered and left again. But by the 9th century, they had begun to conquer and settle in the lands they attacked.

In this scene Viking farmers are shown harrowing the land, then scattering seeds and ploughing them into the ground. Farm machinery was drawn by oxen and mules.

 Farmsteads see page 16

Farmers

Despite their fearsome reputation, most Vikings lived peaceful lives as farmers. Each farm had a longhouse, where both the farming family and their animals lived. Farmsteads were often grouped together to form small villages.

Viking Homelands

Most of Norway and Sweden were covered by mountains and forests. Denmark was flatter, with more farmland. Since the inland areas were often rugged and inhospitable, most people lived along the coasts. The sea was an important source of food. As travel was easier by boat, the Scandinavians became skilled sailors early on.

The time just before the Viking Age is known as the Vendel Period (7th–8th centuries). Wealthy aristocrats at that time wore beautiful jewels like the one shown here.

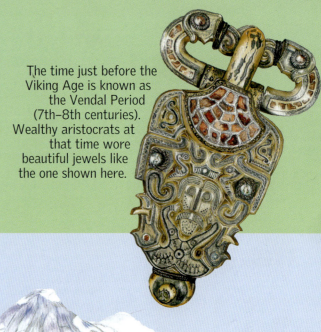

The illustration shows a Viking settlement in Norway. The countryside was rugged, with tall mountains and many lakes.

Human Sacrifice

Human sacrifice was common in pre-Viking times. The victims were placed in peat bogs along with other offerings to the gods. The chemicals in the bogs have preserved many of these bodies. One, known as Tollund man (right), was found in Jutland. The rope used to hang him is still slung around his neck.

Viking Origins

The first people settled in Scandinavia at the end of the last Ice Age. These early people lived by hunting, fishing and gathering plants, but by 4000 BC they had begun to grow crops and raise animals. For thousands of years, the ancestors of the Vikings lived as farmers. Gradually their settlements grew and some powerful local kingdoms emerged. They had contact with the rest of Europe, especially through trade.

Becoming Vikings

The people of Scandinavia developed their Viking characteristics in the second half of the Iron Age, from about AD 1–AD 800. The population increased at this time, and important building projects show that some tribes had become wealthy and well-organized. Many forts were built. Since there were no invasions, this suggests that there may have been a struggle for power among local peoples.

Timeline

Some key dates in the history of the Vikings:

790s: Vikings begin raids on Western Europe

841: Vikings settle in Dublin, Ireland

885–6: Vikings besiege Paris, France

860–920: Vikings settle in the Faroes and Iceland

878: King Alfred divides England with Danish leader, Guthrum

911: Viking leader, Rollo, settles in Normandy

c. 980: Eric the Red settles in Greenland

c. 1000: Leif Ericsson discovers North America

1016–35: The Dane, King Cnut, rules England

1075: Last Danish invasion of England

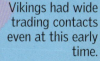

This little statue of a Buddha was made in northern India in the 6th or 7th century. It was found at Helgö, in modern-day Sweden. This shows that the Vikings had wide trading contacts even at this early time.

Targets

At first the raiders attacked undefended abbeys and settlements. Later, when they had become better organized, the Vikings attacked large trading centres and towns. In 885–6 they even laid siege to Paris. They also began to colonize and settle in the areas they attacked. This led to ongoing warfare with local chiefs and kings.

This 12th-century painting shows Vikings approaching the coast of England in their longships.

Lindisfarne

The first raid happened in 793, when the Vikings attacked the English abbey of Lindisfarne, on an island off the coast of Northumbria in northern England. Isolated and remote, the abbey was an easy target. Like other monasteries and churches, it had no defences and was full of precious objects.

The illustration (below) shows the Vikings attacking the abbey of Lindisfarne. Many monks were slaughtered or drowned and church property was stolen or damaged.

This bronze casket inset with precious jewels was found in Norway, but it originally came from an Irish abbey.

Warriors and Weapons

Viking warriors were greatly feared so they must have been very fierce. They were well-armed, with battle-axes, swords, spears, bows and arrows and daggers. Wealthy raiders wore simple metal helmets and chain-mail shirts and carried shields.

A chess piece representing a berserker warrior. Berserkers were a special class of warriors who were said to bite their shields in their violent rage.

Viking Raiders

Viking raids on Britain, Ireland and Europe began in the 790s. People were terrorized by the violent "Northmen" and many thought they had been sent by god to punish them. Without warning, sleek Viking longships appeared on the horizon and warriors attacked unarmed monasteries and villages. The Vikings killed people without mercy and carried off prisoners to be sold as slaves. They stole everything of value.

Why?

The Vikings probably began raiding because they knew from their trading journeys that there were valuable objects in easy-to-attack places. When they began to settle overseas, it may have been because the population had grown rapidly in their homelands and they needed space. Powerful local kings may also have made life difficult for some people and they preferred to live elsewhere.

Bow and arrow

Quiver full of arrows

Dagger

Fully-armed Viking warrior, with battle-axe, helmet and shield.

Swords were used to slash at the enemy. The hilt was often decorated in gold or silver.

On the open sea the Vikings may have used wooden sun-compasses (right) with 32 points to work out in which direction they were sailing.

Navigation

When possible, the Vikings sailed along the coast and did not require instruments to know where they were going. When they made long journeys on the open sea they used their experience of sea and weather conditions to judge direction and distances. In the stormy North Atlantic they were often blown far off course. It is believed that Iceland, Greenland and North America were all discovered by Viking sailors who had lost their way.

If the Vikings ran into a storm at sea there was little they could do. Shipwrecks were common.

Types of Boats

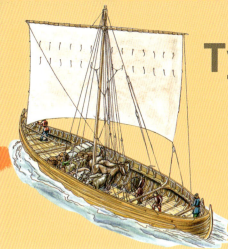

There were two main types of boats: warships and traders. The warships, called longships, could zip along at 10 knots (20 km/12 miles per hour) and were fitted both with a sail for the open sea and oars to manoeuvre in coastal waters and rivers. Trade ships were shorter and wider, with deeper hulls for storing cargo.

A trading ship with domestic animals and cargo.

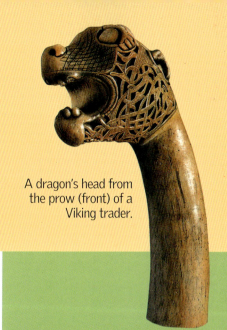

A dragon's head from the prow (front) of a Viking trader.

At Sea

Scandinavia is surrounded by the sea and the land itself is rugged, making overland travel difficult. The Vikings became the most skilful sailors in Europe out of necessity. When the population increased and the political situation became difficult in the 9th century, entire families with all their possessions, including domestic animals, set sail. They settled in lands across the North Atlantic, from the Shetland Islands, to the Faroes, Iceland, Greenland and, finally, to North America.

Shipbuilders at work on a boat.

Decoration

The Vikings decorated the high prows (fronts) of their boats with carved patterns or figureheads. They were meant to scare away bad spirits and enemies.

Viking traders travelled on all the main rivers of Europe. When they had to change rivers or avoid an obstacle they carried the boat over land (above).

Shipbuilding

The Vikings were the best seamen in Europe and they built the finest ships. They were all built of overlapping planks of wood held together by iron rivets. The hull was made watertight by pressing wool or plant fibres into the spaces between the planks and sealing them with tar. They had a rudder on the right-hand side and a single, square sail.

The Vikings made skates by tying animal bones to their shoes.

On Wheels

The Vikings used wagons and carts to transport goods from place to place. They were simple wooden vehicles, pulled by horses. Their use, however, depended on weather and road conditions.

Carts were often versatile. In winter, when the ground was covered in snow, the bodies of wagons were used as sledges.

Winter Travel

Travel overland was often easier in the wintertime when the rivers and bogs were frozen over and the land was covered in smooth, deep snow. Skis, skates and sledges could skim over the top and they were the best ways of getting around.

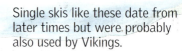

Single skis like these date from later times but were probably also used by Vikings.

Travel and Trade

The Vikings overcame the difficulties of overland travel with practical inventions, such as skis, skates and sledges. Although most trade was carried out over short distances, trade links between Scandinavia and the rest of Europe began to increase during the 8th century. Some full-time traders, especially the Swedes who settled in Russia, made long trading journeys across the rivers of Europe to reach the Byzantine Empire and the Arab world.

Overland Travel

Travelling overland was difficult because of the rugged terrain. The few existing roads were mainly just rough tracks. Most people journeyed on foot, although the wealthy rode horses. Horses were also used to carry heavy loads and to pull wagons, although they could only pass where there were roads.

This tapestry shows people walking, riding on horses and in wagons.

Goods

Viking merchants, most of whom were also craftworkers and farmers, traded walrus ivory, seal skins, fur, grain, timber, iron and other goods with neighbouring countries. In early times Vikings obtained most of their valuable goods through raids and tribute. The Vikings obtained slaves, furs and other goods from their neighbours by force and then traded these for silver with the Arabs.

Viking ships could not transport large cargoes. Goods transported for trade were limited to luxury goods which were high in value but took up less space.

Long-distance Trade

Long-distance trade was made possible by the Vikings' great shipbuilding and navigation skills. The Vikings travelled the Russian rivers to reach the Black Sea and the Caspian Sea. By reaching these seas, they gained access to other trading partners. Once in the Black Sea the Vikings were able to sail across to Constantinople (modern-day Istanbul). When they crossed the Black Sea however, they had to leave their ships on the shore and travel the rest of the way by camel to meet their trading partners in Baghdad.

Payment

Most goods were paid for in silver. Often coins or jewellery were broken into pieces to pay for cheaper goods. Silver objects were usually weighed on portable scales to determine their value. Scales were no longer used after coins with fixed values came into use.

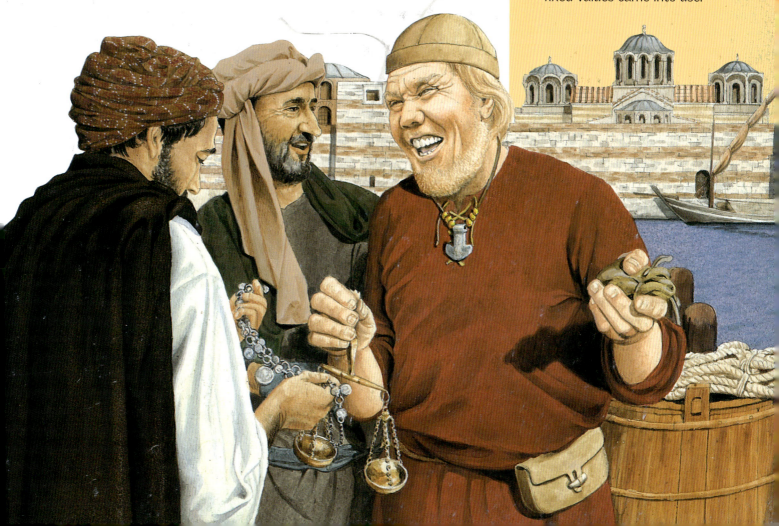

Fishing

Fish and shellfish were a major source of food for Vikings who lived near the sea. They used hooks, spears and traps to catch fish like cod and herring. They also gathered oysters, mussels and other shellfish. Inland, rivers provided trout and salmon. Seals were hunted along the coasts for their meat and pelts.

Fish that was not eaten fresh was smoked or dried to preserve it. Stockfish (above), which is dried cod, became a valuable export for Norway after 1100.

A wine jug (back) and drinking pot (front). Beer was brewed from barley. Mead, a type of wine made with honey, was another common alcoholic drink. Wine made from grapes was imported from the south of Europe and was a luxury only the wealthy could afford.

Farmsteads

Farming was a family affair, and everyone had their tasks. Men usually did the heavy farmwork, such as ploughing and sowing new crops, while women and children took care of the animals.

Sheep shears (left) and wool comb (right). Wooden and iron farm tools were all made on the farm. Vikings often built farmhouses grouped together into small villages where one farmer became skilled in crafting tools and instruments.

Meals

The Vikings ate two meals a day, one in the morning and one in the early evening. The food was served on wooden platters or bowls. Knives were used to cut up meat while simple wooden or horn spoons were used to scoop up stews.

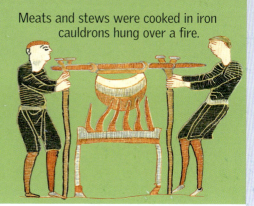
Meats and stews were cooked in iron cauldrons hung over a fire.

Diet

The Vikings ate a varied diet based on plenty of meat, fish, milk, butter, cheese and grains. Meat was boiled in large cauldrons, although it could also be roasted over the fire. Herbs, such as cumin, mustard and garlic, were used to flavour meat.

Vegetables were not an important part of the Viking diet. They used onions and garlic to flavour foods. Cabbage and peas were also served.

Farmers and Food

Almost all Vikings were peasant farmers. Most of them owned the land they farmed, although some were tenants who paid rent to local landowners. Farmers produced almost all the food they ate. Animals, including cattle, goats and sheep, were raised for milk, meat and hides. Oats, barley and rye were grown and made into porridge, beer and a kind of flat bread that was cooked over the fire.

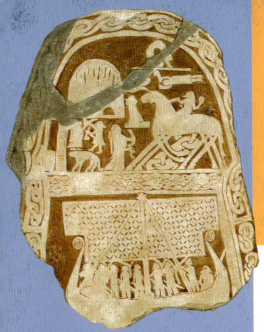

This 9th century rune stone shows Odin on his eight-legged horse, called Sleipnir. The Valkyries are offering him drinks.

The Valkyries

In Viking mythology, the Valkyries were warrior women who lived in Valhalla where they served Odin. They had names such as Battle and Shriek and would swoop over battlefields choosing the warriors who were to die. They took them back to Valhalla where a great feast awaited them. Each day the dead warriors were born anew. They fought all day and feasted with Odin and the Valkyries at night.

Gods and Goddesses

Odin

Odin was the chief god and the other gods served him. He made the world from the body of a giant and set the Sun and the Moon in the sky. Violent and cruel, Odin was the god of battles. He lived in Valhalla from where he could see everything in the universe.

The giant wolf Fenrir was the enemy of the gods who kept him bound in chains. At the end of the world the Vikings believed he would break free and devour Odin.

Before they became Christians, the Vikings believed in many different gods and goddesses. Each one looked after an aspect of human life. Thor, for example, was the god of strength, oaths, thunder and lightning, rain and good weather. He was especially popular with sailors and farmers. The Vikings did not have a holy book and we do not know exactly how they worshipped their gods. We do know that they held festivals and made sacrifices of animals and sometimes of humans too.

Freya

The three most important gods were Odin, Freya and Thor. Freya, the main female deity, was the goddess of love, fertility and marriage. She led an eventful life and was famous for tricking some greedy dwarves out of a beautiful necklace. Freya could turn herself into a falcon and fly, but she usually travelled in a chariot pulled by cats.

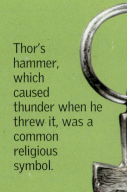

Thor's hammer, which caused thunder when he threw it, was a common religious symbol.

The Valkyries' name comes from the Old Norse and means "choosers of the slain". Here they ride low over a battlefield and point out the men who are to die.

Rituals

Funeral rituals could last for several days, ending with the burial itself. The body of the dead person was treated with great care otherwise it was believed that it could come back to haunt the living.

Jewellery – like this necklace made of glass beads, rock crystals, metal and coloured stones – was buried with its owner.

Brooches, like this one, which were used to fasten cloaks at the shoulder, are among the everyday objects found in burial sites.

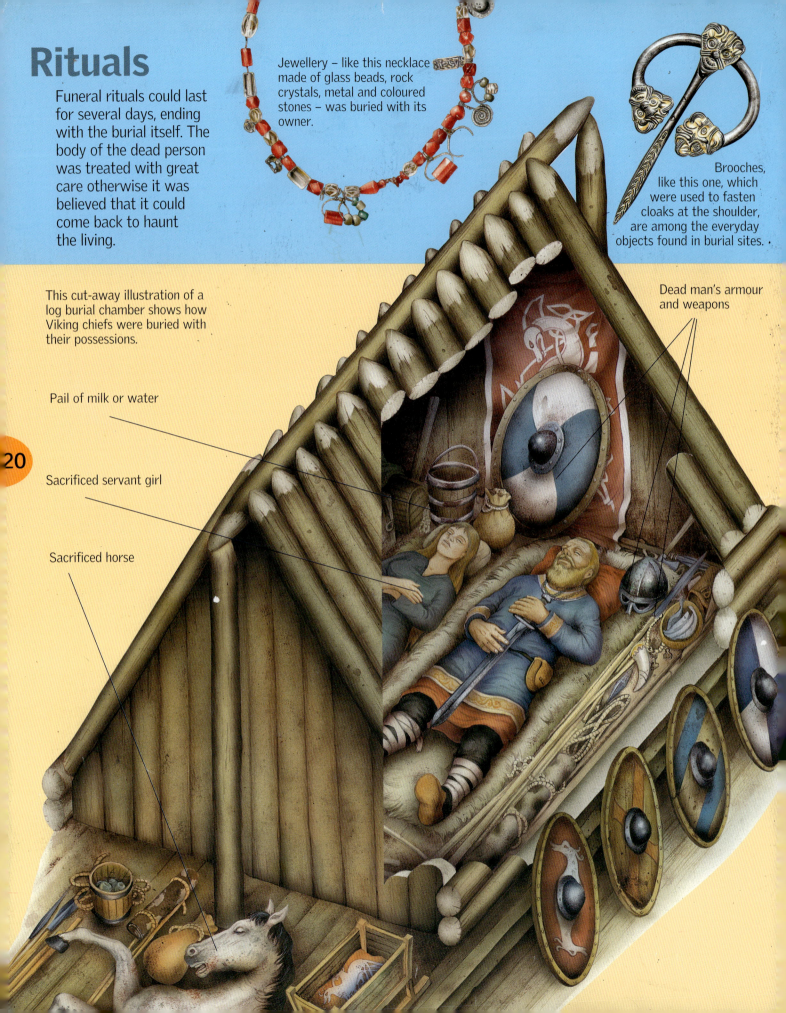

This cut-away illustration of a log burial chamber shows how Viking chiefs were buried with their possessions.

Dead man's armour and weapons

Pail of milk or water

Sacrificed servant girl

Sacrificed horse

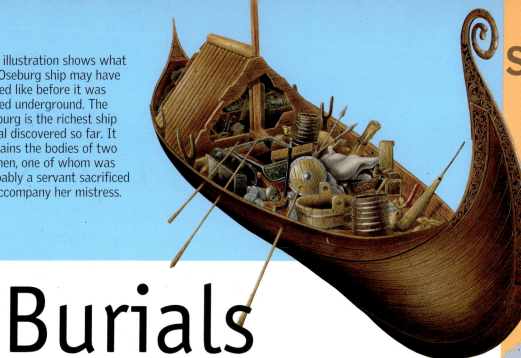

This illustration shows what the Oseburg ship may have looked like before it was placed underground. The Oseburg is the richest ship burial discovered so far. It contains the bodies of two women, one of whom was probably a servant sacrificed to accompany her mistress.

Burials

The Vikings believed that when people died they made a journey to another world. They buried people with grave goods, or possessions (including servants and horses) for life in the afterworld. At the beginning of the Viking Age the dead were usually cremated along with their clothes and belongings. Later, people were buried underground and their graves were marked with mounds. Royalty and very wealthy people were buried in ships.

Ship Burials

Only very rich and powerful people were buried in ships. The boat itself was usually beautifully carved and it was filled with objects from daily life as well as valuable jewellery and other treasures. The richly-dressed body of the dead person was laid out under a wooden covering. Slaves or servants (and often a wife, if the dead person was a man) were sometimes sacrificed to serve the dead person in the afterlife.

The grave stone showing a warrior and his weapons.

This beautifully carved wooden sledge was part of the treasure discovered in the Oseburg ship burial.

Grave Goods

Household utensils, beds, looms and jewellery, as well as food and drink, have been found in Viking graves of the well-to-do. Ordinary people were buried with their clothes and used household objects and old jewellery.

Women's Lives

Women led busy lives, caring for children and the sick and elderly, as well as preparing food for the family. Spinning and weaving wool to make cloth and then sewing it into clothing took a lot of time and effort. Women and girls also milked the cows and churned milk into butter and cheese.

There was not much furniture in a Viking house. Basic items included sleeping couches, tables and wooden stools and chests, like the one shown here.

Inside a typical longhouse, these women are spinning wool into thread, taking care of infants and cooking over the open fire.

Women's graves often contain copies of household keys. This suggests that they were in charge of storing food and other valuables.

Houses

Most Vikings lived in longhouses with their family and animals. Longhouses could be large or small, depending on their owner's wealth. Simple longhouses might be just one room with a hearth, while others were divided into several living areas.

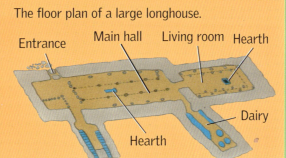

The floor plan of a large longhouse.
Entrance, Main hall, Living room, Hearth, Dairy, Hearth

Children

Childhood did not last very long for Viking children. As soon as they were big enough they began to work on the family farm or business. Girls were taught to spin and weave and helped prepare food and look after younger children. Boys learnt about growing crops and raising animals, or about the craft or business their family was involved in.

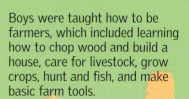

Boys were taught how to be farmers, which included learning how to chop wood and build a house, care for livestock, grow crops, hunt and fish, and make basic farm tools.

Daily Life

The Vikings lived in small, close-knit family groups. Family members were expected to take care of each other and to seek revenge if someone within the family was harmed. Viking society was mainly run by men, who farmed and fished, were craftsmen and traders, and fought in wars. Women were responsible for the home and family farm. Although Viking women had less power than men they had more rights than most women of their time.

This gold foil figure shows a man and a woman embracing. Most marriages lasted, but divorce was allowed. In this case it was enough for the husband or wife to say that they wanted a divorce in front of witnesses.

Marriage

Viking marriages were like business contracts between two families. When a man wished to marry, he (or his father) approached the woman's father to ask permission. If the families agreed, there was a betrothal ceremony and then a wedding feast. The woman went to live with her husband, sometimes in his family home but often in a home nearby.

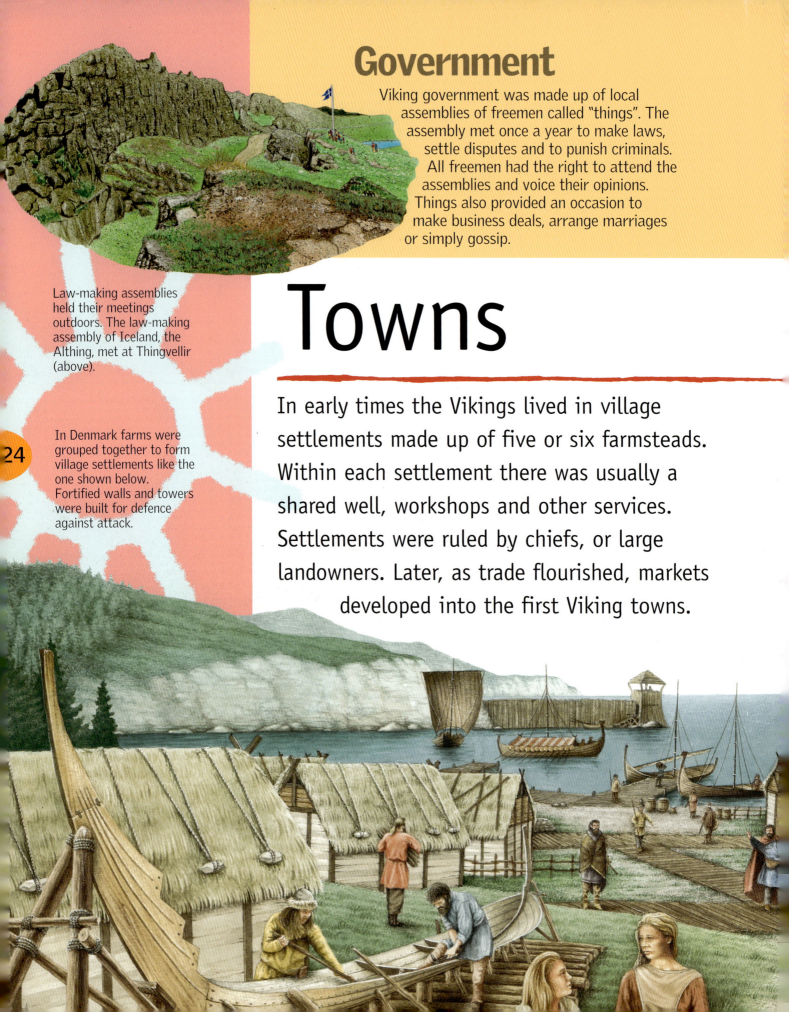

Government

Viking government was made up of local assemblies of freemen called "things". The assembly met once a year to make laws, settle disputes and to punish criminals. All freemen had the right to attend the assemblies and voice their opinions. Things also provided an occasion to make business deals, arrange marriages or simply gossip.

Law-making assemblies held their meetings outdoors. The law-making assembly of Iceland, the Althing, met at Thingvellir (above).

In Denmark farms were grouped together to form village settlements like the one shown below. Fortified walls and towers were built for defence against attack.

Towns

In early times the Vikings lived in village settlements made up of five or six farmsteads. Within each settlement there was usually a shared well, workshops and other services. Settlements were ruled by chiefs, or large landowners. Later, as trade flourished, markets developed into the first Viking towns.

Towns and Markets

At first markets were simple meeting places. Gradually, as workshops and services appeared around markets, they developed into year-round settlements or towns. Some of the first Viking towns were centres founded by kings to secure and control profit from trade through the collection of taxes. The farm settlement of Hedeby quickly developed into a wealthy town when the Danish King Godfred forced merchants to settle there.

A cloth bag filled with weights was used by traders to determine the value of silver coins and objects.

The scene at a Swedish market place, where furs, fabrics and many other goods were traded.

Kings had the authority to issue coins. One silver coin shown here (far right), minted in c. 1000, bears the portrait of King Svein Forkbeard.

Ports

Most markets were established near the sea or rivers to facilitate the transport of goods. Some heavy goods, like wine or timber, were best transported by boat and arrived at ports. Markets which were not located close to a waterway were held only during those months when overland travel was possible.

A rich Viking on his horse holds a falcon while his dogs run on ahead.

Music

We know that the Vikings enjoyed music because of the range of musical instruments that have been found. These include lyres, horns, pipes, bone recorders and an early kind of harp. Musicians and singers performed at feasts. Unfortunately we do not know what Viking music sounded like because it was not written down.

Above: a recorder-like instrument and panpipes.

Hunting

Wealthy Vikings hunted on horseback, with hounds and falcons (tame hawks). Most Vikings hunted using spears and bows and arrows to kill animals that would be taken home to eat. Fishing and birding along the coasts were also popular pastimes that added tasty foods to the home larder.

Sports

Swimming, wrestling, jumping and running races were popular outdoor sports during the warmer summer months. Ice-skating and skiing were enjoyed in wintertime. Games involving bats and balls were played on frozen ponds, although we do not know anything about the rules. The Vikings were keen archers and fencers and they also organized meetings where contestants challenged each other in shows of strength by throwing spears and rocks.

Wrestling matches (below) were often violent and could end in serious injury. Another nasty pastime involved horse-fighting, where stallions (male horses) were encouraged to fight each other.

Games

Dice and board games were popular and helped pass the time during the long, dark winters. The best-known board game was called *hnefatafl* (king's table), a kind of war game that involved soldiers and a king. Towards the end of the Viking Age, chess and backgammon were popular. The Vikings probably learnt chess from the Arabs during their trading journeys.

Feasting
and Fun

The Vikings celebrated by holding feasts. Kings and chieftains gave feasts that could last for several days. Everyone came dressed in their finest clothes and jewellery. Roast or boiled meats were served, along with fish, bread, cheese, vegetables, fruit and nuts. There was plenty of beer and mead on hand and storytellers and musicians kept people entertained.

This *hnefatafl* board was found in Ireland.

Vikings gambled using dice like these. They were usually carved from animal bone or horn.

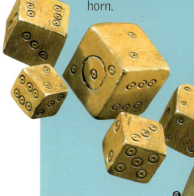

Feasts were served on long narrow tables and guests sat on benches placed on platforms along the walls of long halls.

Wealthy Vikings drank their beer and mead from silver goblets, but most people would have used a small horn, like the one shown here, often without the ornate decorations.

Literature

The Vikings of Iceland composed many stories of the deeds of kings and heroes called sagas. Originally they were passed down orally and recited by poets. They were written down later, in the 12th and 13th centuries. The most famous sagas are historical novels about feuding families during a time of violence and political unrest. The power of fate is a common theme. *Egil's Saga* is one of the best ever written. It tells of the adventures of a warrior, trader, poet and farmer who travels across the Viking world.

An illustration of Egil Skallagrimsson, the hero of *Egil's Saga*, in a 17th-century manuscript.

Sagas were written on sheets made of calfskin called vellum. Books were bound with hard wooden covers.

A 13th-century illustration from a collection of sagas showing the Norwegian king, Olaf Tryggvason, killing a boar and a sea-ogress.

Writing and Myths

The Vikings used a system of writing which involved carving letters into wood or stone. Each letter was called a rune. The alphabet, called the *futhark*, was made up of 16 letters. Since there was not a letter for each sound of speech, spelling was often improvised, making many inscriptions hard for us to interpret.

Runic Inscriptions

The Vikings believed that knowledge of writing was passed down to humans by the god Odin. Runic inscriptions were used to mark ownership of objects, to record charms and curses and to create memorial stones. Short messages were usually carved on twigs. The earliest inscriptions date back to c. AD 150. Runic writing was ultimately replaced with the Latin alphabet after the Vikings converted to Christianity.

Most of the runic writing that has survived comes from rune stones. These carved stone slabs were put up as memorials to dead family members. This stone from Sweden, known as the Rökstone, was put up by a man in memory of his son.

The 16-letter runic alphabet. Runes were made up of only vertical or diagonal lines. Horizontal lines were not used because if the letters were carved on wood they would be hard to read against the grain of the wood.

f u th a r k h n i a s t b m l R

Stories

Storytelling was a favourite pastime and form of entertainment. Professional storytellers were often hired to entertain families. Storytelling was also a way to pass down family history.

A storyteller captures the undivided attention of her grandchildren, as she makes the history of their ancestors come alive.

Christianity

Conversion to Christianity was a slow process. The first missions proved unsuccessful. It was the power of the kings that in the end helped to establish the faith in Viking lands. Conversion in Scandinavia began in the late 10th century among royalty. Kings encouraged Christianity since it helped relations with other kingdoms and united the people, making it easier for the kings to exert their power.

This gold figure, representing the crucified Christ, dates from the 11th century.

Conversion

Before Christianity spread to Viking lands, monasteries and churches were easy prey for Viking raiders. Things began to change however after the Vikings began converting. Those who settled abroad were the first to become Christians. For many years Christianity existed alongside pagan ritual.

Part of the terms of peace settlements for many Viking raiders was conversion to Christianity.

The End of the Viking Age

The Viking Age, which lasted about 300 years, came to an end for several reasons. One of the reasons was the spread of Christianity. As Christianity reached Norway, Denmark, Sweden and Iceland, the Vikings changed their way of life. Also, many Vikings who had migrated to other lands adopted customs of the local culture. The Viking heritage survived however through their descendants, the Normans, who became great conquerors.

This colourful rune stone from Denmark was erected by Harold Bluetooth, a king who converted his subjects to Christianity in c. 960.

A group of Vikings known as the Rus moved east and settled in Novgorod and Kiev. Russia takes its name from this Viking group. Grave goods, such as this silver pin in the shape of a dragon's head, have been found in early Russian settlement sites.

Descendants

In the early 10th century a group of Viking raiders settled in northern France. They accepted land from the French king and in return they converted to Christianity and promised to defend France from other Viking attacks. By the end of the century, their descendants, the Normans, had conquered England, southern Italy and Sicily.

Churches

The earliest Christian places of worship in Scandinavia were built in the 10th and early 11th centuries. These churches were built from wooden planks, called staves, following local tradition. In Norway churches of this type continued to be built into the Middle Ages and the builders developed elaborate designs and fine wood carvings.

The 12th-century church at Borgund, Norway, is one of the few examples of stave churches that still stands today.

A mosaic portrait of Tancred, the last Norman king of Sicily.

Index

afterlife 21
Althing the, 24
animals 7, 16, 17, 18, 22, 23, 26
Arabs 14, 15, 27
Atlantic Ocean 6

Baghdad 15
beer 16, 17, 27
berserkers 11
Black Sea 15
boats/ships 6, 13, 15, 21, 25
Borgund 31
Britain 7, 11
Buddha 9
Byzantine Empire 14

Caspian Sea 15
children 22, 23
Christ 30
Christianity/Christians 18, 29, 30, 31
churches 10, 11, 30, 31
coins 15, 25
Columbus, Christopher 6
Constantinople (Istanbul) 15
crafts 7

Danish/Denmark 7, 8, 9, 24, 25, 30
Dublin 9

Egil's Saga 28
England 9, 10, 31
entertainment 26, 27
Europe 6, 7, 9, 11, 13, 14, 16

family 22, 23, 28, 29
farming/farmers 7, 9, 16, 17, 18, 23
Faroes 9, 13
feasts and festivals 18, 26, 27
Fenrir 18
fishing 9, 16, 26
food 16, 17, 22, 27
France 31
futhark 28, 29

games 27
gods and goddesses 18
 – Freya 18
 – Odin 18, 29
 – Thor 18
government 24
graves 20, 21, 22
Greenland 9, 12, 13

Hedeby 25
Helgö 9
houses 22, 23
hunting 9, 26

Ice Age 9
Iceland 9, 13, 24, 28, 30
India 9
Ireland 11, 27
Iron Age 9
Italy 31

jewellery 7, 8, 20, 21, 27
Jutland 9

Kiev 31
kings 9, 10, 11, 25, 27, 30
 – Alfred 9
 – Cnut 9
 – Godfred 25
 – Harold Bluetooth 30
 – Olaf Tryggvason 28
 – Svein Forkbeard 25
 – Tancred 31

Latin 29
laws 24
leaders
 – Eric the Red 9
 – Guthrum 9
 – Leif Ericsson 9
 – Rollo 9
Lindisfarne 7, 10
literature 28

markets 24, 25
marriage 23, 24
mead 16, 27
Middle Ages 31
music 26
mythology/myths 18, 28

Normandy 9
Normans 30, 31
North America 6, 9, 12, 13
North Atlantic 12, 13
Northumbria 10
Norway/Norwegian 7, 8, 10, 16, 28, 30, 31
Novgorod 31

Old Norse 7, 19
Oseburg ship 21
Paris 9, 10
ports 25

raiders (*see also* warriors) 10, 11, 30, 31
rituals 20, 21
Rökstone, 29
runes 28, 29
rune stones, 18, 29, 30
Rus, the 31
Russia 14, 15, 31

sacrifices 9, 18, 20, 21
sagas 28
sailing/seafaring 6, 12, 13
Scandinavia 6, 7, 8, 9, 13, 14, 30, 31
sea 8, 12, 13, 25
servants/slaves 11, 15, 21
Shetland Islands 13
shipbuilding 13
ships *see* boats
Sicily 31
Skallagrimsson, Egil 28
Sleipnir 18
spinning/weaving 22, 23
sports 26
storytelling 27, 29
Sweden/Swedes/Swedish 7, 8, 9, 14, 25, 29, 30

taxes 25
things 24
Thingvellir 24
Tollund man 9
towns/settlements 8, 9, 24, 25
trade 14, 15, 25
transport 14, 25
travel 14, 25

Valhalla 18
Valkyries 18, 19
Vendal period 8
Viking Age 7, 8, 21, 27, 30

warriors 7, 11, 21
weapons 11, 20, 21
women 16, 18, 21, 22, 23
writing 28, 29